Tear-jerkers

IMP

International MUSIC Publications

Series Editor: Chris Harvey

Editorial, production and recording: Artemis Music Limited
Design and Production: Space DPS Limited

Published 2003

RESPECT THE VALUE OF MUSIC

The First Time Ever
I Saw Your Face

Words and Music by Ewan MacColl

Verse 3:
And the first time ever I lay with you
I felt your heart so close to mine
And I knew our joy would fill the earth
And last till the end of time my love
And it would last till the end of time my love.

Hello

Words and Music by Lionel Richie

Track 3
Backing

If You Don't Know Me By Now

Words and Music by Kenneth Gamble and Leon Huff

It's My Party

Words and Music by John Gluck,
Wally Gold and Herb Weiner

Stay With Me Till Dawn

Words and Music by Judy Tzuke
and Mike Paxman

Slow tempo

The Way We Were

Words by Alan Bergman and Marilyn Bergman
Music by Marvin Hamlisch

Track 7
Backing

What Becomes Of The Broken Hearted

Words and Music by Paul Riser,
James Dean and William Weatherspoon

When A Man Loves A Woman

Words and Music by Calvin Lewis
and Andrew Wright

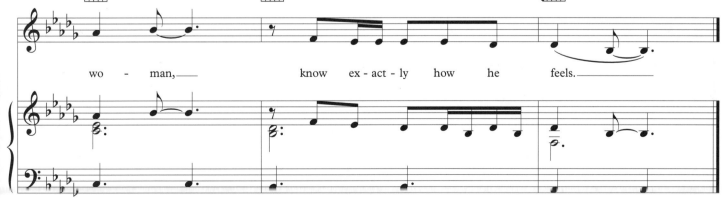

When I Need You

Words and Music by Carole Bayer Sager
and Albert Hammond

Backing

Will You Love Me Tomorrow

Words and Music by Gerry Goffin
and Carole King

Moderately

YOU'RE THE VOICE

8861A PV/CD

Casta Diva from Norma - Vissi D'arte from Tosca - Un Bel Di Vedremo from Madam Butterfly - Addio, Del Passato from La Traviata - J'ai Perdu Mon Eurydice from Orphee Et Eurydice - Les Tringles Des Sistres Tintaient from Carmen - Porgi Amor from Le Nozze Di Figaro - Ave Maria from Otello

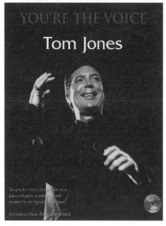

8860A PVG/CD

Delilah - Green Green Grass Of Home - Help Yourself - I'll Never Fall In Love Again - It's Not Unusual - Mama Told Me Not To Come - Sexbomb Thunderball - What's New Pussycat - You Can Leave Your Hat On

9297A PVG/CD

Beauty And The Beast - Because You Loved Me - Falling Into You - The First Time Ever I Saw Your Face - It's All Coming Back To Me Now - Misled - My Heart Will Go On - The Power Of Love - Think Twice - When I Fall In Love

9349A PVG/CD

Chain Of Fools - A Deeper Love Do Right Woman, Do Right Man - I Knew You Were Waiting (For Me) - I Never Loved A Man (The Way I Loved You) I Say A Little Prayer - Respect - Think Who's Zooming Who - (You Make Me Feel Like) A Natural Woman

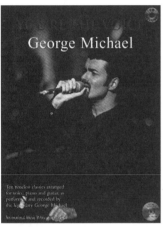

9007A PVG/CD

Careless Whisper - A Different Corner Faith - Father Figure - Freedom '90 I'm Your Man - I Knew You Were Waiting (For Me) - Jesus To A Child Older - Outside

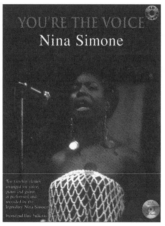

9606A PVG/CD

Don't Let Me Be Misunderstood - Feeling Good - I Loves You Porgy - I Put A Spell On You - Love Me Or Leave Me - Mood Indigo - My Baby Just Cares For Me Ne Me Quitte Pas (If You Go Away) - Nobody Knows You When You're Down And Out - Take Me To The Water

9700A PVG/CD

Beautiful - Crying In The Rain - I Feel The Earth Move - It's Too Late - (You Make Me Feel Like) A Natural Woman So Far Away - Way Over Yonder – Where You Lead - Will You Love Me Tomorrow You've Got A Friend

Frank Sinatra

9746A PVG/CD

April In Paris - Come Rain Or Come Shine - Fly Me To The Moon (In Other Words) - I've Got You Under My Skin The Lady Is A Tramp - My Kinda Town (Chicago Is) - My Way Theme From *New York, New York* Someone To Watch Over Me Something Stupid

9770A PVG/CD

Cry Me A River - Evergreen (A Star Is Born) - Happy Days Are Here Again - I've Dreamed Of You - Memory - My Heart Belongs To Me - On A Clear Day (You Can See Forever) - Someday My Prince Will Come - Tell Him (duet with Celine Dion) - The Way We Were

9799A PVG/CD

Boogie Woogie Bugle Boy - Chapel Of Love - Friends - From A Distance - Hello In There - One For My Baby (And One More For The Road) - Only In Miami The Rose - When A Man Loves A Woman Wind Beneath My Wings

The outstanding vocal series from IMP

CD contains full backings for each song, professionally arranged to recreate the sounds of the original recording

Karaoke Classics
9696A   PVG/CD   ISBN: 1-84328-202-X

Back For Good - Delilah - Hey Baby - I Will
Always Love You - I Will Survive - Let Me
Entertain You - Reach - New York, New York -
Summer Nights - Wild Thing

Party Hits
9499A   PVG/CD   ISBN: 1-84328-097-8

Come On Eileen - Dancing Queen - Groove Is In
The Heart - Hi Ho Silver Lining - Holiday - House
Of Fun - The Loco-Motion - Love Shack - Staying
Alive - Walking On Sunshine

Disco
9493A   PVG/CD   ISBN: 1-84328-091-4

I Feel Love - I Will Survive - I'm So Excited - Lady
Marmalade - Le Freak - Never Can Say Goodbye
- On The Radio - Relight My - Fire - YMCA - You
Sexy Thing

Celebration Songs
9733A   PVG/CD   ISBN: 1-84328-241-0

Anniversary Waltz - Auld Lang Syne – Celebration
– Congratulations - God Save The Queen - Happy
Birthday - Happy Birthday To You - My Way - The
Best - We Are The Champions

all Woman

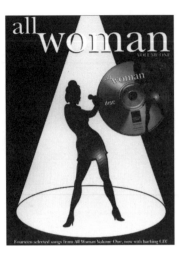

**ALL WOMAN
VOLUME 1 PVG/CD 7077A**

All Woman - Cabaret - Can't Stay Away
From You - Eternal Flame - Ev'ry Time We
Say Goodbye - Get Here - I Am What I Am
I Only Want To Be With You - Miss You
Like Crazy - Nobody Does It Better
The Rose - Summertime - Superwoman
What's Love Got To Do With It

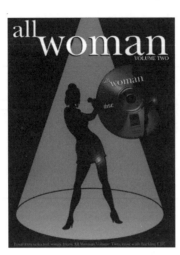

**ALL WOMAN
VOLUME 2 PVG/CD 7268A**

Anytime You Need A Friend
Don't It Make My Brown Eyes Blue
Flashdance....What A Feeling - I'll Stand
By You - Killing Me Softly With His Song
One Moment In Time - Pearl's A Singer
(They Long To Be) Close To You - Think
True Blue - Walk On By - The Wind
Beneath My Wings - You Don't Have To
Say You Love Me - 1-2-3

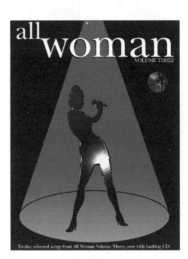

**ALL WOMAN
VOLUME 3 PVG/CD 9187A**

Almaz - Big Spender - Crazy For You
Fame - From A Distance - My Baby Just
Cares For Me - My Funny Valentine
The Power Of Love - Promise Me
Respect - Take My Breath Away
Total Eclipse Of The Heart

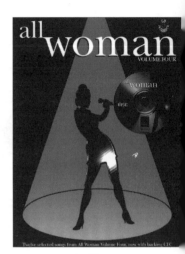

**ALL WOMAN
VOLUME 4 PVG/CD 9255A**

Baby Love - Diamonds Are Forever -
Evergreen - For Your Eyes Only - I Will
Survive - If I Could Turn Back Time - I'll
Be There - Rainy Night In Georgia - Send
In The Clowns - Smooth Operator - Sweet
Love - Touch Me In The Morning

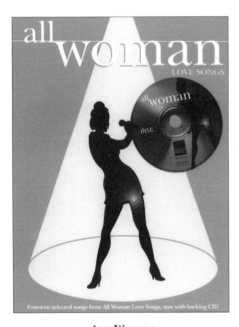

**ALL WOMAN
LOVE SONGS PVG/CD 7502A**

All At Once – Anything For You –
Because You Love Me – Crazy For You –
Didn't We Almost Have It All – The
Greatest Love Of All – Here We Are –
Hero – How Do I Live – I'll Never Love
This Way Again – Saving All My Love For
You – Think Twice – The Wind Beneath
My Wings – Without You

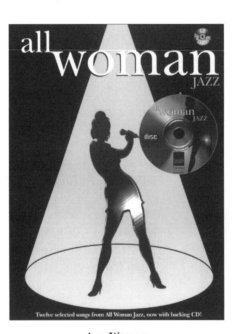

**ALL WOMAN
JAZZ PVG/CD 9500A**

Bewitched – Dream A Little Dream Of Me
A Foggy Day – The Girl From Ipanema
I'm In The Mood For Love – In The
Mood – It Don't Mean A Thing (If It Ain't
Got That Swing) – Misty
Nice Work If You Can Get It – On Green
Dolphin Street – 'Round Midnight
Where Or When

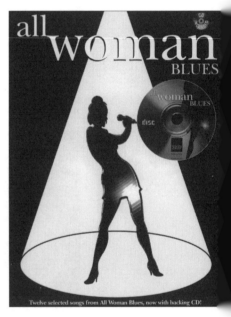

**ALL WOMAN
BLUES PVG/CD 9550A**

The Birth Of The Blues - Come Rain Or
Come Shine - Embraceable You -
Georgia On My Mind - Knock On Wood
Mood Indigo - Night And Day - Rescue Me
Someone To Watch Over Me
Stormy Weather
Take Another Little Piece Of My Heart
What Is This Thing Called Love

Available from all good music shops